THE MOTHER PRINCIPLE

HEALING ALL WOUNDS ...
NURTURING ALL NEEDS

By

GINGER GRANCAGNOLO, Ed.D.

Bloomington, IN Milton Keynes, UK

authorHOUSE®

First published: 08/03/2006

ISBN: 1-4259-5084-1 (sc)

Library of Congress Control Number: 2006907217

Printed in the United States of America
Bloomington, IN

This book is printed on acid-free paper..

Dedication

To Holy Mother God, Blessed Mother, Theotokos, Mary, Shekinah, Lady Nada, Kwan Yin, and to Great Spirit of Mother Earth;

May the true Goddess Light replenish our souls that we might know and feel how much we are loved. Then, having been nourished by Her Loveliness, all humanity can become wholly healed again.

Acknowledgments

To my great-grandmother, Rosaria; my grandmothers, Nana Angelina and Nana Mary; and my mother, Mama Novena, for their cast iron will and determination to push forward, regardless of circumstances or adversity, and make life a celebration, no matter what.

To my circle of prayerful friends, who have always come together as a fortress of love and laughter to create compassionate healing whenever it was needed. They have made me whole.

Contents

Introduction

Perhaps there is no single word more powerfully charged than the utterance "MOTHER." As we say the word openly or silently, emotions and experiences can seek to ruffle our attention, awareness, and acknowledgments.

Whenever we earnestly stop and deeply examine our relationship with mother and/or mother-figure types, it can feel like a wind whirling through an old personal diary that carries the pages out into the open air.

Wait, wait, cry our hearts. What did those pages say? What did I really feel? What really happened? What was written on those pages of my soul's memories? Was the mothering real? Was I abandoned or controlled? Did she really love me?

The truth of these questions can be seemingly lost, just like the diary pages blowing in the wind. Sometimes, we can feel that way about our mother's influence. Sometimes, we are her deep-set clones, and sometimes, it is mother's lingering confusion that continues to shape us.

No matter what the reason, there has always been so much emphasis placed upon the role of mother. In some families, she is revered whether she deserves it or not. Yet, for others, being a mother is an ongoing struggle of work, hope, quiet moments of pain and prayer, countless experiences of unreciprocated love, and a heart rich with wisdom that always seems to heal any conflicted moment.

What is it about being a mother that is so vital to our being and our inner stability? Why is it that we can be brought to such rage or to the purest love because of this inescapable woman in our lives? Whether they are near or far, good mothers or not, with us or released to the justice of heaven, MOTHERS shape and reshape us, over and over, by their thoughts, deeds, love, or omission.

Mothers and mother figures are divinely designed to be our first relationship. Mother's womb is our first security experience. Her body is our source of life. It literally feeds our every need. It is no wonder that this first relationship and "first love" can easily manifest so many patterns, core values, and beliefs. No wonder first impressions are lasting!

Perhaps with this understanding of mother as the cornerstone of our personal development, we can see the need to grasp the ironic impact that most of us have verbalized. In good times or bad times, proudly we defend, "Just don't talk about my mother!"

Even though this human response to mothering, mother or the absence of her nurturing in our lives is remarkably significant, the importance and the Divine purpose for having a mother is even more powerful than we can imagine.

Just as the seedling, newly ejected from its pod, enters the world with the assurance that there will be soil, so too the infant expelled from the womb approaches life on the assumption that it will be provided for by the mother. For the mother is to the child what mother earth is to the seed—without her, it would perish.[1]

Our mother-child attachment, connection, and union are essential to the promulgation of life, our life, and ultimately evolution itself. No wonder we have so many mother issues!

The Divine purpose for this essential union is called *the Mother Principle*. Within each of us and written upon the soul is the message of mother.

The Mother Principle that ripples out of us through our inherited "mother message" is this: inner security. Although this may seem simple and quite a traditional impression, the true effect of the Mother Principle expressed in our lives permeates every emotion, behavior, and relationship.

The purpose of this book is to allow for a safe inward journey, so that the mother mold within us can be reviewed, assessed, accessed, and appreciated. Regardless of the quality, mother's love shaped the quality of the security in our hearts.

My own mother molds are a mixture of old-world Italian-American homemaking wrapped in an unusual twist for the modern-day woman, released from her apron.

Great-Grandma Rosaria gave birth to sixteen children, nine of which lived full-term lives. She couldn't read or write, yet upon her death it was discovered that she had her own bank account. Grandma had been renting the abandoned garage across the street from her house for years. She had secured a plump amount of

[1] Dr. Anthony Stevens, *Archetypes* (New York: Quill, 1982), 85.

money on her own "just in case the family" needed it. Her daughter, my grandmother Nana Mary, went to school and was married at age sixteen. She continued to study in the textile industry and became one of the first female buyers in Hahne and Company (Hahne's Department Store) in Newark, New Jersey.

Nana's nickname was Mary Ma. There was always some extended family person living in the house. She gave these people helpings of love, stability, and discipline. She held onto their money to prevent frivolous spending. When they were ready to leave and go out on their own, all the savings were returned without a penny missing.

My paternal grandmother, Nana Angelina, was stately and beautiful. She had five sons and taught them all to wash and iron their own clothes. She, too, was Italian born, yet became Americanized and learned to drive the family Buick. Papa was adamant about teaching his sons to honor, obey, and respect their mother. Nana Angelina taught me my first prayers in her native tongue. She would speak to me in Sicilian and I would answer her in English. I loved her big, warm hugs. She made me feel safe.

So, if you are ready to safely venture into your heart's deepest treasure, let us begin and let us pray the following:

O Holy Mother of the Universe

Protect us in this journey; Let Your

Radiant Light create waves of Love

To ripple through us, as we move

Out of the world of shifting distractions

And into the silence of our own Soul,

Pulsating with Your Peaceful and Serene Care.

In You we are safe, forever.

Chapter One: Who Is Your Mother?

As we begin this deep, insightful reflection, let's imagine that it is a few days before Mother's Day, or some significant holiday, and you are in search of the perfect card to express your sentiments for your mother. Imagine you are in the card store and reading card after card, trying to choose the right one that really captures what you believe and feel at this moment.

Have you ever noticed that your feelings about that holiday message can change from season to season? Sometimes, you select a simple, to-the-point, not-too-wordy, yet pretty card. Other times, your decision can bring you to tears even before you get to the register to pay for it!

Why did that happen? How can one woman cause so many emotions? The answers to these questions are pivotal to the understanding of who your mother and mother-figure types really are. Regardless of how your mother is presently connected to you, her influence remains paramount in all your relationships, especially the relationships you are having with yourself.

So, who is this woman? Did you feel safe in her presence? What did she do with her emotions? What did you feel if you saw her cry? Did you see her pray? Did she teach you how to pray or how to be comfortable in silence? Are your memories about mom or mother-figure types filled with emotional confusion? And, perhaps most importantly, what did you do with that confusion?

One of the purposes of this book is to help you to embrace this inner confusion, to go deeper into your feelings, and to grasp the Divine reason behind the mother-child dynamic. Through this reassessment, you will become aware of the ongoing influence of the Mother Principle in your life.

The Mother Principle is an active energy within you. It is meant to assist you in becoming emotionally safe and secure no matter what your external reality may be. The Mother Principle as defined by Carl Jung in a 1909 dissertation is a core archetype within each person that holds truth energetically within the subconscious.[2] This innate template breathes in you like an active living disposition. The Mother Principle archetype functions like a living organism, endowed with generative force. It has the capacity to initiate, control, and mediate your common behavioral characteristics and experiences, and oftentimes without your awareness. The purpose of the Mother Principle Life Force is to get you to feel, connect, reconnect, change, heal, and ultimately transform yourself completely from inside out. These effects all get triggered in you, based on who your mother is/was to you and how you responded to her dynamics. In pure essence, the Mother Principle energy can be identified as Mother Nature, Mother Earth, Goddess of Fertility and dispenser of nourishment, Vessel of Life, Water Love, Creation. She is all Life, especially the invisible, the unconscious, and she is the font of all

2

intuition. The Mother Principle is the Feminine Face of God in all Her Divine Power and has also been named as Blessed Mother, Theotokos Shakti, Shekinah Azna, Juno, and Athena. Some of Her best manifestations can be felt through music, poetry, cooking, dancing, gardening, praying, and all the healing arts.

The Mother Principle is deeply woven to the experiences of the intangible world. How you use, trust, or mistrust your instincts and how you convert your emotional responses into personal growth and inner security are the direct result of how you are allowing the Mother "within you" to have Her way with you.

All power to transform is always available. This precept and the relationship dynamic with your mother and mother-figure types set the tone for the measurement of your own emotional common sense. Somewhere, early on, you and your mother began a relationship pattern that may or may not be serving your soul's thirst for freedom, joy, and love.

Although this pattern may appear to be out of reach and nearly impossible to change, relax! Peace, healing, and comfort permanently breathe within you. Through the use of the following "Prayer Room Exercise," you will be able to feel instinctively more alive and internally more secure.

The easiest way to create your "Prayer Room" is to just take a few moments now and follow the process.

---

[2] Stevens, *Archetypes*, p. 39.

Prayer Room Exercise

- Be comfortable, in a sitting position.

- Adjust your body so you can remain quiet for a few moments.

- Close your eyes and take three deep, slow breaths.

- With eyes closed for the rest of this exercise, imagine you are at the top of a staircase with ten golden, lighted, descending steps.

- Continue to descend each step, slowly, even feeling the Golden Light ascending up your legs, through the soles of our feet.

- Take your time, and continue to breathe deeply and slowly as you count from one to ten silently to yourself.

- At the count of ten, you will be at the base of the staircase, standing in a silver-lighted doorway.

- Now, at the count of three, you will pass through the silver-lighted doorway, saying silently to yourself, "I seek peace."

- One, two, three. Now you are in a room that shall be called your "Prayer Room."

- Be very creative—decide all dimensions, floor, ceiling, walls, and color.

- Create a skylight in the center of the ceiling to allow an imaginary beam of blue-white light to connect you to the center of the universe.

- You may say silently here, "As above, so below."

- Create a comfortable chair, lounge, etc. that you sit in every time you are in your "Prayer Room."

- Create the proper lighting that pleases you.

4

- Create where this "Prayer Room" is; imagine it to be in a private wooded area, near a lake, or a get-away beach house on a remote tropical island.

- Be freely creative! This is your personal, private "Prayer Room."

- Create flowers, fountains, open, spacious windows with a beautiful view.

- Be certain to remember that the center beam of blue-white light is the Life Force that is always connected to you. It is the very Power and Presence of God.

- Now be relaxed, sitting in your chair, and allow the blue-white light to wash all over you, even through you.

- Repeat several times, silently, "Peace, peace, peace."

- Now just listen and trust your first impressions; just let the experience be, without judgment.

- Feel, sense, your personal responses …

  - Do you believe that there is the Power Source of All Life, always breathing within you?

  - Can you feel/sense the Power, know that Power, and let it just relax you?

  - Do you know that your breathing, every breath, is the Breath of God? You are always breathing the Divine Source of Peace, Joy, Healing, no matter what, simply because you're breathing, by day and by night, unaware or aware the Power breathes in you, always, now and always.

- Continue to relax, breathing the blue-white light in an easy, steady manner, in and out, occasionally repeating to yourself, "Peace, peace, peace."

- Whenever you are ready to complete these prayerful moments, just say "thank you" and walk back through the silver-lighted doorway, then ascend back up the ten steps of Golden Light and back out to outer conscious awareness.

- Then open your eyes, more relaxed and at peace with yourself.

This Prayer Room exercise will be used at the end of every chapter with a particular healing function in mind.

Chapter Two: Mother Love and the Curse of Mystification

The irony of love is best exemplified in the union of mother and child. This loving bond is revered, protected, and can be a source of undetected dysfunctionality in most adults. This paradoxical process begins in utero.

As the Spirit of our unborn self is creating bone and flesh through the Divine Power of our Creator, our beings and environments are safe, self-contained, and self-regulating. All these simultaneous miracles are housed in the protection of our mothers' wombs. This safety is divinely ordained and so the feeling of security and love becomes our first innate experience. This is the true nature of God as Divine Mother, who chooses to wrap us in a protected sheath of the Holy Spirit. Her Holy Essence is breathing our part of the divine plan with every beat of our newly formed, tiny hearts. The Will of God is etched into every vertebra and is impressed within us as deep as DNA and cellular memory. Truly we felt as close to God as we were to the rhythm of our mothers' souls.

Through this experience, our souls "knew" heaven and earth are one. The union of mother and child knew no boundaries or divisions. The feeling of flow was felt to be us. It was total bliss.

Somewhere within nine months this ecstasy was abruptly halted as we were expelled from our mothers' wombs. According to

9

our birth conditions, our souls now feeling their own body had to process new feelings of temperatures, light, sounds, and a variety of tactile experiences just to get us to have a first bath! These interactions become life's first lessons and cognitions that would continue to shape our individuality for the rest of our lives. For much of the first year, human life may therefore be regarded as a post-uterine embryonic phase. Such a degree of helplessness renders the mother absolutely indispensable. She is the baby's life support system in a dangerous, inhospitable world.[3]

The relationship with our mothers is absolutely life giving and life regulating. Perhaps at this stage it is natural to take for granted all of the efforts of this personally administering angel. After all, during the first year of our lives, she is the promise of our existence. It is only at the end of this phase that a "relationship" becomes possible. At this point, our attachment bond has secured a repertoire of behaviors that we will use later to express our needs that can be recognized and satisfied by our mother.

The next stage is composed of the ages one to about three years old. During this time, we are attempting to distinguish ourselves from our mother and others. This is our first challenge. The dilemma is how can you keep a safe bond with mother and develop connections with others in the family without losing a sense of safety? This becomes the cornerstone lesson of life and love: trust vs. mistrust.

---

[3] Stevens, *Archetypes*, p. 86.

That first bonding with our mothers and the blissful feeling of "mystification" is no longer promised or assured. This gift is now available only after much discernment. We continue to grow and live in a variety of circumstances; some are safe and some are not.

If this stage has not been properly developed, the "curse" of the mystification sets its impression. Having no guarantee of that flowing, trance-like feeling, once known as our home (mother's womb), our newly developing personality may become stuck in emotional confusion. The subconscious self poses questions and reflections about who, what, when, and how it can feel safe and validated. If a child's every feeling, thought, and desire is being controlled and measured, this little person soon learns "the only time I am loved is when I am doing what someone else expects."[4] This baseline incongruent construct, therefore, translates into the adult who chooses not to be the true self for fear of painful invalidation. Believing we are lovable only when we are not being ourselves results in what is termed by John Bradshaw (*Creating Love*) as toxic shame. Toxic shame becomes the deep dark void inside us that never seems to go away. Somehow we always feel that there is something wrong with us and in our very being.

According to David Hawkins in his book *Power vs. Force*,[5] the emotion of shame generates the lowest frequency of life force energy. It makes us feel like we are running on empty because we feel almost empty of self-love.

---

[4] John Bradshaw, *Creating Love* (New York: Bantam Books, 1992), 6.
[5] David Hawkins, *Power vs. Force* (California: Hay House, Inc., 1995), 68.

Shame disconnects us from God. We feel barren of Light, Love, and Purpose. Our souls cry out "I am not enough." So once again we seek to enmesh in someone or something in order to stop the pain and reclaim that trance-like union we had just before birth.

This search for mystification can drive us into despair, a string of unhealthy relationships, no intimate relationships, and the false belief that God has abandoned us.

The healing of mystification begins when we reclaim the truth that is always present within us. God has a feminine face and She is our Divine Mother forever. Only when we can allow ourselves to feel the loving Presence of Mother God in us and around us by day and by night can we begin to feel our true worth as our Creator intended for us to enjoy it.

Only the loving encounter of Mother God, who always knows us personally, can heal the false void and allow us to see ourselves as whole, complete, "not damaged goods."

If you are ready to dissolve the confusion set in by the illusion of feeling separate, I invite you to enter into this prayerful exercise.

Prayer Room Exercise: Dissolving the Illusion of Separation

- Use the same procedure to enter into your Prayer Room as outlined in Chapter One.

- Take your time, repeatedly breathing in and out in an easy, rhythmic manner.

- Be more aware and creative with the design of your Prayer Room.

- Add any details you desire—color, texture; use all your senses to enhance the experience—sight, hearing, taste, smell, touch.

- Allow yourself to be sitting in your chair or lounge now and sense the Blue-White Light from above pouring all around you, even through you.

- Now relax and listen inside yourself to your responses to these questions.

- Be honest, spontaneous, without judging the experience.

- Imagine and sense your mother to be right in front of you; feel her presence and just observe her; take your time.

- What is the first feeling you feel? Is it positive? Negative?

- Is this a usual, common feeling for you to have of her?

- Continue, as much as possible, to stay focused on your feelings.

- Now allow your heart to release several random flashbacks, five years ago, ten, twenty, as far back into early childhood as possible.

- Take your time and pause as long as you like for any one memory; allow for any and <u>all</u> emotions.

- As you are re-viewing these Mom scenes, repeat often to yourself, "Peace, peace, peace."

- Now, just trust your first impressions.

- How are you most like your mother?
- What did you most dislike about her?
- Do you feel guilty or ashamed in having these negative feelings about her?
- Are you free to just be yourself with her?
- What do you do when you don't feel safe?
- Were you hugged freely by your mother?
- Did you have to earn her attention and affection?
- Was your mother ill, bedridden, or absent at any time during your early childhood?
- When you are alone, do you feel safe? Sad? Or do you have to keep busy?
- Do you feel confident to express your emotions with others? Or do you fear rejection and invalidation?
- Do you feel lonely even when you are with someone?
- What do you do when you are lonely?

- Take your time feeling and silently responding to each question.
- After completing all questions as clearly as you can, then pause for a moment to allow a sense, a vision of the Feminine Face God to be present to you.
- Sense Her Pure Divinity and open, outstretched arms.
- Sense a Magnificent Violet Light and Silver Light radiating from Her Heart to yours.
- Feel your heart open and shielded in this God Light.
- Ask Mother God to heal all abandonment, all shame, and all feelings of loneliness.

- Ask Her, Blessed Mother of all, to be your mother for the rest of your life.
- Ask Her to wrap you in the Light of Pure God and re-create inner calm and safety in you permanently.
- Stay in this feeling as long as you like; even become a child if you choose to.
- When you are peaceful and ready to do so, simply conclude the exercise by saying "Thank you" and ascending the ten steps of Golden Light, back out to outer conscious awareness.

It is advised that you complete this exercise several times. Your awareness increases every time. It is also good to write feelings and/or responses in a journal for further reflection.

Chapter Three: Needs, Wants, and Addictions

Somewhere inside of us, we long to enjoy the pleasures of life, like the feeling of a well-satisfied, full belly. Our modern society may call this a "driving force" for success. Our peers can positively or negatively motivate us to enjoy the "good life." Yet, it appears, for many, that we are always searching. We are striving for the perfect or right career, partner, house, retirement plan, body weight, hair style, and car model. Perhaps the western culture is the best example of this constant, unquenchable yearning to feel fulfilled.

If we are to be honest, most of us have a piece of this driven personality or an addiction to functioning as part of our daily routine. We are addicted to our coffee, clothes, hairdresser, cyberspace, comforts, and basic habits of how we eat, sleep, have sex, and go to work. We push through the day into night, sometimes wishing we were somewhere else, or maybe even going home to someone else. If we took a survey involving just our close friends and family to ask the simple question, "Are you happy?" I think the responses would invoke more questions and answers. We might respond: "Well, compared to whom or what?" "How can anyone be happy in this violent world?" or "Sometimes I am happy, but it doesn't seem to last."

All these responses serve a valid point about how we develop with regard to the Mother Principle. The truth is while in the womb we were safe, loved, protected, and fed both by mother's body and Mother God's Love. The soul knows this inner template for fulfillment is still there. In quiet moments, alone or in intimacy, we yearn for the connected feeling. We instinctively know it exists and is available. However, the deeper questions are: How can I sustain being fulfilled? Does love really last? How do I know whom to trust?

In the silence of the heart, our soul can feel the power of the Divine template and is reassured we were designed and meant to remain one with God, one with Love. However, daily grinds of multitasking to survive without truly thriving make this truth quite evasive. Here lies the source of unsatisfied, addictive lives. Our spirit remembers the feeling but doesn't know how to release this potential into everyday living. We have real moments of fulfillment as opposed to a life of perpetual soul-enhancing peace and joy. In fact, if someone did express such happiness, we might retort, "Are you on drugs?"

Through these emotional conflicts, the inner seesaw begins. The result is a pattern of dependency vs. independency. This hole in the soul seems to push us to attach to persons, places, beliefs, and substances for stability and security. Life's road then becomes paved with vulnerability and addictions, all because we don't feel we are "enough." It is this feeling of inner lack that fosters the addictive personality. Addictions occur when we place a meaning upon a person, place, belief, or substance that in fact it doesn't inherently have in and of itself, in order to feel a certain way. For example, we may assign a false meaning to cigarettes, such as smoking looks cool or important. We may assign a significance to a job, such as "This will make me feel powerful." We may desire a particular partner as if it were the promise of prestige. In all these cases, we will feel satisfied for a while, yet this feeling is certain not to last. Addictions are counterfeit replacements for feelings we falsely believe we do not inherently have the power to create on our own.

This false vs. real seesaw can distort the true self and hide deep wounds of insecurity, depression, and anger. Emotions are so powerful that they can drive a life into integrity and value or into unfulfilled potential and dreams.

The key to this dilemma is found by unlocking the functions of addictions, needs, and wants. Our true nature is a constant yearning. In the Divine sense, this is a necessary urging so that we can evolve and mature into our godlike nature as promised by God. Every desire can fuel us into potential and greatness. Desires, however, can be left unsatisfied, thereby yielding perpetual grief and frustration. It remains a matter of choice coupled with intention. Whenever we seek to fulfill a desire, need, or want and we follow counsel from our Divine Heart, we are more likely to be enhancing the soul's delight and purpose. However, when needs are satisfied from outside fulfillment, we inevitably will drive an even deeper stake into an already gaping wound of fear and lack. Satisfying ourselves without taking into consideration the self as a mind-body-spirit unit is a prescription for disappointment.

Our desire nature is a sacred ambiguity. Whenever we desire to be, do or have anything, a spark is ignited inside. To complete any task, goal, or want, we need to fire up motivational energy to get there. This is good. This is the unfolding of God's creative power inside seeking to burst forth in newness and success. Such activity rebirths us into our own unique evolution. It gives witness to God's proclamation, "You are made in My image and likeness." Thus, when we create desires and their accompanying satisfactions, the feeling of God is released through our very veins. We become enlivened and reinforced in Mother God's Love. We feel safe and empowered again.

Desire keeps the promise of evolution alive. Intentions without Divine Mother Guidance, however, perpetuate the path of personal lack that can lead to ultimate despair. Without attending to the messages in emotions, we can be led into an obscure reality of egotistical allurings with no substantial grounding in Divine truth. As stated by Neale Donald Walsch, "Feelings are the language of the soul."[6] The soul is Divine Mother's womb. As a perfectly loving mother, God waits for us to come to Her in private and in safety. This is the reminiscent peace felt in our earthly mothers' bellies.

The act of birth and early life experiences thrust us out of the safety of the womb, earthly and divine. Depending on our biological

---

[6] Neale Donald Walsch, *Conversations with God. Book I* (New York: G. P. Putnam's Sons, 1995), 45.

mothers' (or mother-figure types') ability to create such an emotionally protected environment, our ability to use our desire nature can become thwarted. Desires may inadvertently use us. Trusting our own power to create satisfaction of needs and wants becomes veiled and seemingly unavailable. Even during infancy, the young soul can sense if mother hears the cries correctly! These early experiences shape the beginning of a lifelong relationship rooted in these starter desire days of trust vs. mistrust. The mother mold imprints the heart and soul very early. And the shaping and reshaping, having desires fulfilled or not fulfilled, continues for a lifetime.

The mother mold positive and negative is not to be judged but hopefully rather observed for awareness and growth. For there is no perfect mother, only our Divine Mother from within.

If you are ready to clear the illusion of trust and mistrust as they relate to your desire nature, I invite you to enter into this prayerful exercise.

Prayer Room Exercise: Reclaiming Desire and Trust

- Use the same procedure to enter into your Prayer Room as outlined in Chapter One.
- Take your time, repeatedly breathing in and out in an easy, rhythmic manner.
- Be aware of how you feel in your Prayer Room.

- Let yourself create whatever you need to assure a good and safe feeling whenever you are in your Prayer Room.

- Add any details to enhance safe feelings; use all your senses.

- Allow yourself to be sitting in your chair or lounge now, and sense a brilliant Violet Flame from above pouring all around you, even through you.

- Now relax and listen inside yourself to your response to these questions.

- Be honest and spontaneous, without judging the experience.

- Recall a recent desire, goal, need, or want you may have had.

  - What were your immediate feelings as this idea came to you?

  - Did you feel exhilarated? excited? revitalized? hopeful again?

  - Then what happened? Did this feeling get interrupted with some negative beliefs or expectations?

  - Did you hold onto your dream or desire and seek a plan to create it into fruition?

  - Or did you crush the possibility, thinking you were not able to make it happen?

  - Did you check your true intentions for this desire? Is it ego based or soul based?

  - What do you think this will do for you once you get it?

  - Does this desire perpetuate your addictive pattern personality? Or does it enhance your soul's desire to be more godlike?

- What do you think will happen if you don't get this desire met? Is it ego based or soul based?
- Do you feel you can satisfy any need or want because your desire nature is aligned with the Divine Heart of God?
- Or do you feel you are in competition with others, life or yourself to "prove" something to someone or yourself?
- As a child, what did you do with your needs, wants, or desires?
- Did you express them, ask for assistance, or keep them to yourself?
- Did you develop any addictions—smoking, drugs, caffeine, alcohol, sex, cyberspace, work, pleasing others?
- Have you connected any awareness about early experiences with your mother, mother figures, and being safe on your own?

- After completing all questions as clearly as you can, then pause for a moment and allow your senses to create and imagine a vision of the Feminine Face of God to be in front of you in a brilliant Violet Light.
- Sense Holy Divine Mother God in this Violet Light and see Her weaving Her Violet Light directly from Her Heart to yours.
- Continue to breathe in and out until you can actually feel your heart pulsating in the same Violet Light.
- Now observe Holy Mother as She shows you an image in Her Heart that is an image or photo of a particular experience in

which you may or may not have had your desires, needs, or wants manifested in the way you would have liked to occur.

- Ask Holy Mother to release the truth about this experience so that you can understand how to live from your heart and soul and not merely your head and ego.

- Ask Holy Mother to show you how early experiences with your mother and mother-figure types were meant to shape your soul into true self-empowerment, even if these early times felt unloving or mistrusting.

- Ask Holy Mother to show you times in your life when your mother or mother-figure types gave you opportunities to feel safe and satisfied.

- Stay in these feelings as long as you like in order to grasp true understanding.

- Whenever you are ready, conclude the exercise by saying "Thank you" and ascending the ten steps of Golden Light, back out to outer conscious awareness.

It is advised that you complete this exercise several times. Your awareness increases every time. It is also good to write your feelings and/or responses in a journal for further reflection.

Chapter Four: The Power of Change

The nature of the "Father Principle" as it reflects God as Father is to be the Truth, the Masculine Force, the Intellect, the Constant Force or Prima Mobile. So, too, does the nature of the Mother Principle resonate with a specific function in our lives. The Mother Principle reflects Mother God. She is the all-powerful "giver of life who pervades the cosmos like a mother bird hovering over the primordial chaos" (Genesis 1:12). She shelters those in difficulty under Her wings (Psalm 17:8) and bears up the enslaved on Her great wings toward freedom (Exodus 19:4). Like a mother, She knits new life together in the womb (Psalm 139:13); like a midwife, She works deftly to bring about the new creation (Psalm 22:9-10); like a washerwoman, She scrubs away bloody stains of sins (Psalms 51:7). These and other such symbols invoke the exuberant, life-giving power of women.[7]

These rich metaphors release the Mother God archetype from within us. The Mother Principle is the deep wellspring of all human emotions. This is the pure, explosive nature that creates the dramatic experiences in our life for better or worse. The Mother Principle bursts forth in us in positive power and/or negative.

The true function of the Mother Principle in us is not just emotion for emotion's sake. It is much more Divine in design and purpose. The Face of Mother God deeply embossed in our souls is meant to allow us to change! She moves us, pushes us, even forces us to change and evolve. This inhale and exhale of life-giving Spirit is also created through the mother mold. More precisely stated, the mold our mothers and mother-figure types have made upon us causes us to transform.

Our mothers are designed to be the closest relationship, as well as our first relationship. We must remember the term mother mold is quite exact. For nine months, we were "molded" as one. We were fed from the same life-blood as food. We felt each other's soul even before we knew each other's name. After we were born, our mothers were designed to continue our shaping by being the main focus for our life support and security. As infants, our eyes darted through shapes and a sea of faces. Where is she? Where is she? Where is the one whose sound and smell and breath gave me life? This connection is the essence of the mother mold. And again, for better or worse, she sculpts our emotions, motivations, securities, and insecurities. Mothers are meant to move the heart and soul into action. Just as ancient, spiritual, and mythological symbols of Empress Power, High Priestess, Hera, Kwan Yin, Blessed Mother, Shakti are depicted as the Transformers, Healers, Forgivers, Nurturers, and Creative Force of the Universe, mothers are the source of our emotional development. As powerful as she is, we learned by example or the lack of it. It is for this reason that I

---

[7] Sylvia Brown, *Mother God* (Carlsbad, CA: Hay House, Inc., 2004), 52-53.

describe the mother mold in this capacity as the "Gift of the Divine Irritation."

No one can influence us more dramatically than our mothers! Mother knew us even if we didn't think she did, even if she didn't respond like she did. How could she not? We once shared one body. Fathers shape our ability to go out into the world, while mothers mold our ability to go into the inner world and feel safe and loved. None of our mothers were perfect. This, too, is part of the Divine Plan. Mother's job was to light the Divine spark within us, to foster feelings and reactions of all kinds. The mother-mold relationships made us angry, ashamed, guilty, safe, inspired, neglected, abandoned, confident, and afraid. Mother did exactly what she was supposed to do—irritate us! She did it with a look, a phone call, or no phone call. She did it with a loving surprise, endless lectures, unmentioned prayers, and inaudible praise. She was the constant grain of sand in our lives that promised endless strings of Divine Pearls according to what we did with all those emotions! All this was so instinctive because she is one with the Mother God who is the force behind all change.

Our mother-mold relationships were handcrafted to rub us the right way and the wrong way in order to get us irritated enough so we would have to do something. Mother Principle energy causes us to take actions. According to the quality of these responses, we can become more drawn to the inner world of our soul. We can ask more profound questions and seek deeper answers for life, rather than plodding along stuck in societal expectations, promising only that history will once again repeat itself. Relationships with our mothers and mother-figure types create opportunities for real feelings that can be powerful enough to cure a disease because they can cause us to plummet into the vast unknown, even into the "dark night of soul." Then we can finally find the true unconditional love of God ever present in our own beings.

Mothers are designed to motivate soul-size transformation. Even though any unearthing from within can be life altering, mothers can push the change through mundane urgings, both knowingly and unknowingly.

Such an urging brings me to a personal mother-mold experience. So many times my mother would ask me the same simple question over and over. With pushing inquiry, I could feel the range of emotions go from high to low and back again. These probing questions seemed so unreasonable to my young ears. Why does she want to know? (Please note I would never refer to my mother as "she" in the presence of my father! An emergency dental appointment would have been in order.) What does "she" want from me? It wasn't until much later, and probably in a menopausal moment, that I realized my mother wasn't asking me questions with such diligence for her information; it was to stimulate my discernment and to build wisdom. My mother made me look deeper, sometimes whether I wanted to or not! What a blessing! What would I have become without her holy Divine Irritation?

Regardless of how we may have assessed the love we received from our mothers and mother-figure types, the purpose remains the same. The mother-mold relationship is meant to move us deep within so we can eternally feel the Feminine Love of God as Healer, Changer, Evolver, Transformer, and Holy Mother who answers all petitions when spoken to from our hearts.

If you are ready to feel the effects of your mother-mold relationship and how it may have motivated you to change your heart, then continue graciously by entering into the following Prayer Room Exercise.

Prayer Room Exercise: Teach Me to Change

- Use the same procedure to enter into your Prayer Room as outlined in Chapter One.
- Take your time, repeatedly breathing in and out in an easy, rhythmic manner.
- Allow yourself to take your time and notice every breath, really letting yourself release more and more stress with each exhale.
- Allow yourself to be sitting in a comfortable chair or lounge and sense a brilliant Violet Flame from above pouring all around you and even through you.
- Create an image of Mother God to be a certain comfortable distance in front of you.
- Create Her as beautiful, loving, nurturing, and all-caring and sense Her to be in a flowing Blue-White Light.
- Sense Her connecting Her Love Light directly into yours, as if it is being woven back and forth from Her to you.

31

- Now allow an image of your mother and/or mother-figure types to be there also. Allow your mother to be facing you and let the Blue-White Light from Holy Mother God flow through your mother as well.

- Now continue to just breathe and become very aware of any and all emotions without judgment.

- Now be honest and spontaneous and allow yourself to explore the following questions.

- Take your time; you are wrapped in Holy Mother's Divine Love throughout this experience.

  - Can you recall a "Divine Irritation" that caused you to change in a particular way, due to how your mother interacted with you?

  - Can you recall both positive and negative "irritants"?

  - What were the emotional responses that you experienced because of these "irritants"?

  - How did they alter your ideas, perceptions, life decisions?

  - How did you feel towards your mother and mother-figure types because of these "irritants"?

  - What did you learn about emotions or feelings because of these situations?

  - Did these experiences create opportunities for you to learn more about prayer and spirituality?

  - Did these experiences create opportunities for you to explore and discover more about your own inner strengths, talents, compassion, and courage?

32

- After taking ample time to respond to these questions, take a few more deep breaths and allow your attention to remember, focused upon the image of Mother God.

- Continue to feel Her Holy Presence and ask Her to speak to your heart about why you were born to this woman called mother (mother-figure type if adopted).

- Ask Holy Mother to open your heart so you can understand how all of your mother's strengths and weaknesses were meant to motivate a powerful change in you that would serve your growth and others.

- Ask Holy Mother to help you to communicate to your mother if you desire to speak directly to her spirit regardless of whether she is on earth plane or has already moved on.

- Then ask Holy Mother to help you to hear with your heart any message that your mother may have for you.

- If you choose to, allow yourself to embrace your mother, as Holy Mother God holds both of you in Her loving arms.

- Take your time and just "be" in this experience.

- Then note the changes you may feel from this prayerful meditation.

- Whenever you are ready, simply conclude this exercise by saying "Thank you" and ascend the ten steps of Golden Light back out to outer conscious awareness.

It is advised that you complete this exercise several times. Your awareness increases every time. It is also good to write your feelings and/or responses in a journal for further reflection.

Chapter Five: Relationships—Right vs. Real

Perhaps the best-known love story is that of Romeo and Juliet. As we explore this relationship just a few layers deep, we begin to unfold the hidden power of love, even if it means "until death do us part." These prolific young lovers were willing to risk it all as they reached toward their idealistic dreams to be together, while realistically, due to parental influence and rejection, they were doomed.

We search for love, and sometimes, more importantly, we yearn to feel loved. Yet we can all relate in some ways to the tragic love story of Romeo and Juliet. Our searching for good, solid relationships can be a driving force in our lives. Often we even temporarily find it. We marry, divorce, then try again. We marry, feel loved, have children, and the original love seems to spin off into some other intense drama inundated with bills, responsibilities, and daily-life pressures. Modern-day marriages of good substance often have to resort to a day planner, or even worse a "palm pilot," in order to schedule an appropriate time for intimacy! Young love rarely matures into the elder love so epitomized in the book and movie, "The Notebook." The deep cut of incongruence here is that we are born and designed to love and be loved. It is truly innate in our nature since our Creator is the Divine and Eternal Essence of Love itself. As we breathe, so does Godly love breathe with us.

Even though we are always one with Love, our families, relationships, and friendships struggle with highs and lows, control patterns, and the pain of betrayal. These inconsistencies are the source of the Divine Irritation that the mother mold initiates.

Because our first relationship was with our mothers, how mother's love or the lack of it was experienced could presuppose the script for our adult love lives. Mother's style of love for her sons and daughters sets the mold for future love, which will always include the Divine Irritation. It is important to note here that this original love impression is not intended to be blameful or accusatory. Quite the contrary! Her style promotes self-development through her moods, miscommunications, deep passions, talents, and demands.

Mothers bond differently and for different reasons with their sons and daughters. It is how mother bonds that creates the relationship mold that we typically repeat in our own adult ways of loving. Mothers can bond to their sons in ways that are positive or detrimental. A negative mold can be formed when a mom can no longer connect to her husband because of stress, work, or loss of intimacy. She then connects to her son as a surrogate. She makes him feel extra special. She focuses more attention and "protection" towards him than is necessary or healthy. Her son becomes her main source of interaction in her life. She may even proudly state, "We are so close." Parents are not friends—and mothers and sons are not meant to be incestuously intertwined.

This dysfunctional pattern invariably produces an adult "irritant" for the male. He will eventually become resentful towards women as relationship after relationship does not satisfy what he thinks he needs, based on how his mother treated him. With awareness, he will discover the destructive hidden contract that was made with his mother. He was to satisfy her adult void with emotional discourse, even though he was still an immature boy, and in return, mother would make him feel important. The horrid glue of this contract is veiled control and selfish manipulation. As the boy becomes the man, protection of these ills will sicken good love into relationship melodrama and mutual crazy-making.

Sometimes this mother mold creates a true personality disorder known as misogyny.[8] Misogynistic men demonstrate a negative mother mold. These men were raised by mothers who controlled, rejected, abused, or suffocated them. The result was a malformed concept of love between men and women. These men fear their boyish immaturities and inadequacies. They also fear the women they love, thinking the bond will be reminiscent of the mother mold. Known or unknown, this kind of mother mold falsely makes men feel unloved for whom they really are and loved for how they can be "used" by women. Men in these patterns will engage in whirlwind courtships and display rageful outbursts without warning. These men are wounded by mothers and dwarfed in their true capacity to truly love and be loved. They were robbed of their

[8] Susan Forward, *Men Who Hate Women and the Women Who Love Them* (New York: Bantam Books, 1986), 8.

ability to properly develop the male and female aspects of themselves because their mothers' patterns interrupted the natural course of development.

This is not to decide a dismal path of doom and despair. In proper light, this "Divine Irritant" can reveal an opportunity for these "boys to men" to really heal themselves and the future of men. The hidden pearl can be prized when this classification of males seeks the Feminine Face of God from within through prayer (and counseling in some cases) so that he can reclaim his real value for who he is on his own merit and motivation. His life can become a stellar example of a "real man" who uses power not force.

Conversely, a positive mother mold can be formed even if it didn't seem to be so loving. The major difference comes from the intention of the mother's true heart and soul. A positive mother mold between mothers and sons develops when the mother understands that even if there is a strong, loving connection, her job is to push her son into emotional independence. This occurs when she keeps her word for rewards or consequences and does not accept useless negotiation of new terms simply at the whim of the child. This mother mold remains the parent, teaches respect of all life by example, and sets boundaries that declare everyone in the household is to share in chores and responsibilities. She expects her son to succeed because she really believes in who he is. She prepares him for an adult emotional life by allowing daily challenges in life to be accepted and dealt with rather than "protecting him" from getting frustrated. She teaches by example that he is not weak or victimized by life's unexpected occurrences no matter how great or small. She teaches him to believe, trust, and pray to an Absolutely Loving God that lives inside him and who will never let anything happen to him. This strong and loving mother demonstrates hope, joy, and wisdom even in the face of utter disaster. Her life exemplifies courage and faith from her belief in God's Love. As this mother mold unfolds, the man then develops inwardly and is prepared to celebrate his life emotionally and responsibly. He is sensitive to his feelings as well as those of others. He can maintain an in-charge attitude for his path. We feel safe around this kind of man. He is genuinely good.

I recently observed a wonderful example of such a balanced man. While on a ski vacation to Salt Lake City, I decided to stretch my skills on the slopes, so I signed up for a ski lesson. My instructor was an energetic, courteous man in his forties. He immediately assessed my present abilities while making me feel at ease for a fun-filled adventure. We pleasantly chatted on the lift. I could feel his passion and expertise for the sport, even though I hardly knew him. He was kind, expressive, and made me feel safe, as run after run he clearly was directing and bringing me to another level of skiing. It was great. His leadership was encouraging without being overbearing. He made my day and I am an improved skier!

Mothers mold their daughters also, however the shaping creates different relationship patterns. In similar fashion, the mother-daughter bond can cause positive or negative adult development. In either case, there will be a Divine Irritant. In these busy and difficult times, mothers have mutated into somehow believing their being a "superwoman" is a good thing. Perhaps the seedling of human rights spawned into "You've come a long way, baby" was a causal factor. Positively, this movement pushed for equality of all men and women. However, as the family unit transformed into yours, mine, and ours, and divorce rates spiraled, women's and mothers' roles also expanded into boundless proportions. Over the last several decades, mothers have become more than what they were naturally intended to be. Hence, *Women Who Do Too Much*[9] presently looks normal. This kind of mother mold is a working mom, whether she gets paid or not. She is cooking, cleaning, and organizing the kids' soccer schedule, gymnastics schedule, and costly birthday parties, while trying to squeeze in a day at the mall or a yoga lesson. She drinks mocha latte and reads on the treadmill, with an earbud to her cell phone in case "they" should call. Everyone needs her—her husband, ex-husband, the church, the kids, and, of course, her mother. Somehow this mom knows this isn't right and doesn't know how to change it since every task seems important. If this mother has a daughter, she is teaching her how to be an old, worn-out crone way before her time.

Mother and daughter bonding in this multitasking relationship serves to teach daughters either to become exactly the same or get stuck in the "little princess stage." After all, mom will do everything and her daughter will expect her to. This mother mold bakes cookies and finishes the science project for her daughter, even

---

[9] Patricia H. Sprinkle, *Women Who Do Too Much* (Grand Rapids, MI: Zondervan Publishing House, 1992), 14.

if it is 1:00 a.m. She lets the kids sleep in her bed because they won't sleep in their own rooms and she's too tired to do anything about it. This busy mother is concerned if her daughter doesn't dress equally to her sassy peers and inappropriately stresses about her daughter's appearance and weight, while making sure all her accessories appropriately match. Often in common conversation this mother emphasizes the kind of husband her daughter should or shouldn't marry, as if this discernment alone would be the promise of a happy and secure life. These daughters are encouraged to be the best because it will make them feel good about themselves. Inevitably, these young daughters sometimes won't be chosen for the play, cheerleading, or the team, and they won't have enough internal self-esteem to accept it, be upset a little, and move on. Their mothers will often try to appease these growing pains with extra privileges, treats, and shopping. A mother mold of this kind teaches the daughter to stay a "damsel in distress" because she has learned to wield more power and control through its caricature.

Should this daughter choose to marry in her adult life, she is vulnerable to unsatisfying love since she probably will pattern her own parent-child relationship. She'll stay confused about whether women are strong or weak, imitating both, yet never finding her own soul's true purpose. If this weakened daughter learns to reclaim her Goddess energy as co-creator, she'll merit self-reliance, beauty, poise, and grace all in one lifetime. Truly she was born to be ever pregnant with God's Love and Abundance. She should never be stifled. Through the magical gift of storytelling, Clarissa P. Estes proves this point in her famous book, *Women Who Run With the Wolves*.[10] Story after story, Clarissa P. Estes illustrates young girls are to play, dance, explore, discover the Great Spirit of Nature, smell the earth, and let the power of rivers run through them. The mother mold can lovingly do this when the mother herself demonstrates self-approval through self-care activities that are never arrogant.

Sometimes mothers weren't nurtured properly when they were daughters, and these childhood hurts and neglects clearly become apparent in their inability as adults to emotionally care for their own daughters. Their own adult needs overshadow those of their daughters. These daughters become servants, pleasers, and rescuers, always trying to do more, hoping love will be their reward. More doing will never heal the being. Silence in the heart, and choosing God as her mother, will. There in her prayerful soul, she will reclaim her emotions as vehicles through which Loving God speaks. Holy silence becomes her counselor, healer, and mother.

Good positive mother molds for daughters may seem unusual or distinctively unique. Real mothering is a holy, wisdom-filled, spiritual, and profound expression of love. Mothers are created as close to spirit as humanly possible. They hold the creative power that promises every generation is meant to make heaven on earth. Mothers feel the presence of God as they give birth because they ultimately surrender to it as they become a mother. This miracle can speak to them endlessly.

---

[10] Clarissa P. Estes, *Women Who Run With the Wolves* (New York: Ballantine Books, 1992), 7.

Good positive mother molds allow prayer, silence, and reading to be a part of their normal, everyday habits. They live from faith oftentimes without needing to speak of it. Daughters need mothers who believe in the Presence of Spirit from within and who exemplify it. Faithful mold mothers encourage prayer as a reverent connection to an All-Loving God. Prayers are about guidance, listening, healing, and not only for crises and endless petitions. Good mother molds celebrate life intensely and joyfully, even if the road of life is rocky. Positive mother molds deeply know, converse with, and care for their children. However, these mothers do not get absorbed into their daughters' personae, forgetting they have needs themselves.

A positive example for a daughter is the mother who is witnessed as continuously caring for herself through nutrition, yoga, exercise, fun, and romance. This mother mold states elegantly by her actions, "I am of my own woman and not just an indentured servant to others' needs." She knows her power and seeks to develop it, share it, and make a bona fide contribution to her community by her presence. A true positive mother mold speaks with her soul. Her voice is her energy, filled with individuality and grace, and she is heard by her very presence.

When a daughter is raised and influenced by this style of woman, her own life choices are about value, self-respect, and self-love. She will grow and be happy with or without a man.

If you are ready to examine your relationships as they might mirror your mother molds, I invite you to enter into this prayerful exercise.

43

Prayer Room Exercise: Mother's Reflection in My Relationship

- Use the same procedure to enter into your Prayer Room as outlined in Chapter One.

- Take your time, repeatedly breathing in and out in an easy, rhythmic manner.

- You are becoming more and more comfortable being in your Prayer Room.

- You may make any adjustments within your Prayer Room; change details, colors, etc.

- Now imagine the Presence of Holy Mother God in front of you.

- Allow yourself to create an image of Her Divine Self in a way that is appropriate and acceptable to you.

- Sense the Divine Feminine Face as radiant, glowing in Violet and White Light.

- Feel her Presence as Pure Love and Compassion and feel Her directly send Her Light into your heart and soul.

- Divine Mother will now show you a Golden Book of your relationship experiences, similar to a photo album.

- The book is presently closed.

- Continue and take a deep breath and then place your hands on the Golden Relationship Book together with Divine Mother's hands as well.

- Now follow with Divine Mother as She will open the Golden Relationship Book.

- Divine Mother has now opened the book with you and shows an image of a significant relationship person in your life. Focus upon his/her face and just relax.

- You may or may not still be in a relationship with this person.

- Holy Mother is now surrounding you with many angels and archangels to enhance your sense of clarity and understanding.

- Now breathe deeply again and honestly reflect upon the following questions.

  - What attracted you to this person?

  - What was going on in your life at the time you met this person?

  - At that time, did you feel needy, lonely, or sad? Did you feel incomplete?

  - How did this person make you feel about yourself? Did he/she encourage your own growth and development? Or did he/she overtly/covertly seek to prevent it?

  - Did you allow this person to grow and change according to his/her own needs?

  - Could you be quiet, silent together for a while without thinking or feeling there was a problem?

  - Did you openly pray together without there being a crisis or need?

  - Did you talk about emotions easily? Or were there "topics" that were clearly off limits?

  - Did you harbor resentments, angers, fears that never were clearly discussed?

- Did either one of you hold a grudge?

- Did you honestly forgive and forget any hurts or disappointments?

- If there was intimacy in this relationship, did you feel loved and respected?

- Now take a few more deep breaths and ask Holy Mother to open the Golden Relationship Book to the section marked "My Mother Molds."

- Now allow Holy Mother to show you an image of your mother from this particular section of the book.

- Relax and feel Holy Mother surrounding you in Her Loving and Protective Violet and White Light.

- Feel Divine Mother as She speaks to your heart and illuminates it in wisdom, compassion, and awareness so that you can understand how your mother/mother figures influenced your relationship for better or worse.

- Just relax and, if necessary, allow Divine Mother to pour true forgiving Grace through all concerned.

- Then ask Divine Mother to dissolve any and all relationship patterns that you still may have that have in any way prevented you from experiencing Real Love—both given and received!

- Be at peace, all is Blessed; be thankful!

- Whenever you are ready to conclude this exercise, say "Thank you" and ascend the ten steps of Golden Light back out to outer conscious awareness.

It is advised that you complete this exercise several times. You will be amazed. Your inner peace and understanding will increase every time. It is also advised that you record your feelings and experiences in your journal for further reflection.

Chapter Six: Mothers Mothering Everywhere

Perhaps the biggest buzz word for the 21st century is the word POWER. It invokes excitement, victory, success, pride, conquest, liberation, intelligence, and superiority. The word power is used and overused in marketing, advertising, sports, and finances. We try to create our lives to achieve the essence of this word and fear the lack of it. We set goals, employ life coaches, and buy better technology, all in the hope that something will help us to improve ourselves. Meanwhile, our days and nights seem to fill up quickly with tasks, responsibilities, and "deadlines."

Our list of "stressors" can be endless. We worry and toil about too much responsibility, threats to our self-esteem, phone calls, the need to overachieve, family problems, money, traffic, retirement, our sex lives, our friends, and good, old-fashioned uncertainty. These issues flood our minds and our bloodstreams. Male and female alike, we worry about everything and everyone for some reason—real or imagined. This constant river of fear keeps us free floating in a stream of anxiety. Most of the time, this is a huge waste of emotions leading to exhaustion and unproductivity. Our defense to this fear-based kind of living is to "secure" ourselves and loved ones to the best of our ability. This inner drive for power, safety, and protection is directly related to the Mother Principle. As stated earlier in this text, the Mother Principle is the Feminine Face of God that is eternally deep in our souls and is designed to keep us emotionally and spiritually safe and protected, no matter what. It is Divine Mother's Heart that beats within the womb of our own, if we would just stop and listen to Her. In the listening, we would reverently hear "I am with you, you are safe." This is part of our Divine Master's promise for non-anxiety-ridden living.

Unfortunately, the clamor of endless stress from the outside world can deafen us to the sweet music of a peaceful way and our attention stays focused on how we can stop the worldly noise or simply become numb to it.

When we do not know how to feel and hear the Voice of Mother Divine with all Her safe guidance, we become scattered chickens running through our daily lives striving to merely fix things, put out fires, and get things done. The gentle soul who is yet unconnected to Mother's counsel can develop a personality that tries to help, serve, and correct problems. These good-natured men and women can "feel bad" for others without discretion and sometimes even feel responsible for helping others without being asked. Sometimes these individuals are "consumed by a passion for righteousness."[11] For some, this attitude becomes all pervasive. It follows them or actually drives them at work, home, and in relationships. Even though their intentions are good, much unnecessary upset can result. Overprotection of children, codependent control, useless feelings of victimization, and loss of appropriate relationship boundaries become manifest.

The underlying cause for these behaviors is a false belief that one should use power to protect and secure self and others. This belief, however, does exclude a realistic response to true and moral danger. It is meant to explain the knee-jerk reaction that is fear based. When individuals are not grounded in a sound internal mechanism of faith and practical confidence, they can remain in the prison of their fears. These individuals can be "mothering" (or smothering) a person or situation for a seemingly good cause. It can be confusing to onlookers since it initially appears to be so loving, unselfish, and even smart. The counterfeit root, however, is unrealistic fear.

So many people can be vulnerable to these emotional displays because so many are already wounded by the lack of good mother love. Through these compulsions the cycle of mothering, smothering, even meddling can continue.

If we would just pause and breathe for a moment whenever some cautious situation occurs, we would keep the pathway open for Divine Mother's love, guidance, and direction. Unfortunately, if negative habits overrule, the very lifeline we need snaps shut out of an inappropriate fight/flight response.

If we were to just pause and breathe for a moment during a time of need, crisis, or uncertainty, we would be able to feel and follow a basic Divine Truth. God does not work in one person's life without simultaneously working in others' lives to accomplish the same purpose. Every event in our lives is designed to heal us, bring us closer to God, and lift us to our true purpose on earth. What causes us not to hear or

---

[11] Sprinkle, *Women Who Do Too Much*, p. 37.

feel Divine Mother's counsel is fear and control. Out of some kind of fear, we will control. This will choke the Spirit's ever-present message in any needy moment. The Master Plan is the Master's business—not ours! The Plan is always about goodness, love, healing, and forgiveness. For this is who the Master is and it cannot be any other way. What we do have control over is how we choose to respond to life's experiences. We can choose from our humanness and inevitably be stymied by fear, lack of knowing, and uncertainty of outcomes. Or we can bring our humanness to our Divinity and seek perfect direction from Holy Mother, who awaits from within. Her Blessed Nature knows our fears and worries and comforts them. In Her peaceful arms, we become safe and protected again. Then Divine Wisdom can naturally flow through us. Ultimately we are all always safe. It just matters how we choose and if we are willing to stop "pulling" for our way.

To illustrate the plight of mothering, smothering, meddling control, the following poem is here for your delight.

Little Red Wagon
By Kimberlee Ann Burdick

During her tenth summer
she loved playing mommy to baby sister.
Each baby climbed into the little red wagon
pleading for a ride.

Because she loved the cargo
little mommy pulled the wagon.

Looking ahead, she pulled with strong fervor.
After all, baby needed mommy!
Over the summer, it became routine.
Little mommy had found her call.

Summer passed
as did the years.
Because she loved pulling the wagon,
little mommy accepted the cargo.

Looking ahead, she pulled with tired determination.
After all, this was her duty!
But it became a drudgery
and little mommy was exhausted.

Glancing behind, she groaned,
"How did you ALL get in my wagon?
I can't keep pulling much longer."
(Baby sister had been joined by daddy
and mommy and friends and even some strangers!)

Looking bewildered, they all screamed,
"Stop your damned pulling and we'll get out!"

Without realizing it, we pull others because we fear they'll never be able to pull themselves. Pulling, even with the best of intentions, doesn't allow the person to find Divine Mother and be led by Her Infinite Wisdom. Sometimes it's ego that makes our decisions when it ought to be Spirit. Perhaps ego can be a great teacher if we can remember it might mean <u>e</u>dging <u>G</u>od <u>o</u>ut.

The balance of discerning moments can be found when we realize that the true self is always one with Divine Mother. It is the real "I."

Dag Hammerskjold writes:

At every moment you choose yourself. But do you choose your-self? Body and soul contain a thousand possibilities out of which you can build many I's. But in only one of them is there a congruence of the elector and the elected. Only one—which you will never find until you have excluded all those superficial and fleeting possibilities of being and doing with which you toy ... and which hinder you from discovering the talent entrusted to you which is your I.[12]

---

[12] Dag Hammerskjold, *Markings*, translated by W. H. Auden (New York: Alfred A. Knopf, 1966), 17.

Although this may sound negative towards anyone's attempt to help someone, it is not the intent. What is vital about our natural helping instinct for one another is to question and examine what kind of assistance we are delivering. Does one's extension of powerful aid create independence or dependence? This is the core of the issue. Whenever we participate in someone else's life, the best gift of giving is to help them to find their own center. This kind of help is in fact guiding them back home into the presence of Divine Mother that is within them.

It is clear here that that is how the Feminine God does help all of us. It is also clear that our own mother and mother-figure types may or may not have been able to model that image. Please note there is no blame to be pointed towards anyone's mother. Her job was never designed to be "perfect." Her part in our journey was designed to spark the process of finding our Divine Mother on our own. The mother mold was meant to help us make our own inner choices so that we could partake of our real inner source of power and safety.

Sometimes when we review the significant people in our lives, it can feel like an unending tapestry of who made us feel safe and who didn't. Somewhere along the way, we may need to stop looking outside, fearing what might happen, and go inside in quiet in order to reclaim our true and powerful selves.

If you are ready to assess your own ability to access inner strength, confidence, and peace, I invite you to enter into this prayerful experience.

Prayer Room Exercise: "Reconnecting to Divine Wisdom"

- Use the same procedure to enter into your Prayer Room as outlined in Chapter One.

- Take your time, repeatedly breathing in and out in an easy and steady manner.

- Be aware of how comfortable you are becoming every time you enter into your Prayer Room.

- Focus on your breathing as you repeat the word "relax" several times.

- Allow yourself to be sitting in your chair or lounge now and sense a brilliant, soothing Pink Light pouring into your Prayer Room and creating a gentle shower of peace that flows through and around your whole body.

- Now, as you are enjoying this beautiful shower of gentle Pink Light, repeat the word "Peace" to yourself several times.

- Now allow yourself to create an image of Mother God that you feel comfortable with.

- Sense Her in dazzling luminescent light and feel Her extending rays of Peace from Her Heart to yours.

- Now continue to relax and listen inside yourself to your responses to the following questions.

- Be honest and spontaneous, without judging the experience.
  - Who in your early childhood made you feel safe and protected?

- Sense this person now and feel the person sending you his or her love again.
- Did your own mother make you feel safe?
- Sense her in front of Mother God now.
- Sense Mother God connecting to your mother and healing any "hole" in her soul that may have prevented her from mothering you in a safe and protected way.
- If you need to and are ready to, forgive your mother if for any reason she was not able to protect you in those early years.
- Sense the Presence of Mother God, forgiving both of you if need be.
- Now take another deep breath and repeat the word "Peace" to yourself several times again.
- Now relax and honestly answer the following questions.
- Do you feel safe in your present life?
- Do you really believe God is there for you as a Holy Divine Mother ready to help you in any situation?
- Is there an experience or memory that has prevented you from relying on Mother God for guidance and protection?
- If so, are you ready to ask Her to uncreate these negative impressions?
- How do you respond to unexpected events in your present life?
- Do you become afraid? Think the worst?

- Or do you pause and, while honoring your feelings, seek to hear inner guidance from the Spirit of God within you?

- Do you take enough time every day to be quiet and prayerful so that you can skillfully hear the voice of Mother Wisdom?

- Do you pray only in crisis? Do your prayers include praise, forgiveness, and gratitude?

- Do you share your faith experiences with loved ones, family, and friends?

- Do you really believe and trust that every experience is designed by God to "help us" not "hurt us"?

- If not, are you ready to ask Mother God to uncreate the part of you that still fears God isn't really taking care of your needs?

- Continue to breathe deeply; ask Mother God to instill in you the gift of feeling safe in Her care.

- Accept this gift, for it is real!

- Then turn over any present worries, fears, or concerns that you may have. You can even imagine putting them in a beautiful jeweled basket that She is holding. Ask Her to take them away and to give you the gift of peaceful wisdom instead.

- Then, if you choose, ask Mother God to help you to hear Her Wisdom for your life every day.

- Say thank you and accept this gift. It is real.

- Take as much time as you need now and spend it in the Presence of Holy Mother God.

- Whenever you desire, you can simply complete this prayer process. Say "Thank you" and ascend the ten steps of Golden Light, back out to outer conscious awareness.

It is advised that you repeat this exercise several times. Your appreciation for God's Inner Wisdom will increase. It is also advised that you write your feelings and/or responses in a journal for further reflection.

Chapter Seven: Nurturing Your REAL Self

Over the last two or three decades, the theme of self-improvement has become a multibillion-dollar industry. This movement certainly includes books, CDs, lectures, and seminar retreat workshops. It is multicultural and multidiverse in approach and technique, all connected to the same focal point—the importance of taking care of yourself. Millions of people worldwide participate in these ideas at some level. Some use yoga and organic cooking. Others meditate while gardening, and still others suggest golfing is their meditation.

With so many choices, questions arise. Which method is right or best? How does one know if he/she is "doing it" correctly? How does one know if he/she needs to engage in a particular style of self-help?

Before we get specific about the choices to be made, the most important discussion is stimulated by another question: Do self-help approaches really nurture my REAL self? To answer the question, I would like to make a distinction between self-help techniques and nurturing the REAL self. Self-help techniques can assist us in managing our lives and layers of personalities. They can give instructive tips for "de-stressing" or improving image. Such tools can build better communication skills. All in all, they can make us feel better in our world. However, these styles are mere cosmetics in terms of knowing, healing, and nurturing the soul. Some may not even be clear about what or where the soul is! Or does it really exist? Proof of the soul's significance and presence can be demonstrated by the fact that no cadaver ever got off the morgue's table by itself. The soul is the full presence of God and our individual personhood. This union is so closely woven that the very breath we breathe is the ongoing relationship of ourselves and God as one. This Divine coupling is the REAL self. The soul carries in itself the blueprint of all our incarnations and the purpose or plan for each one. The soul contains all our history and the stories written in every moment. Each experience carries with it the spark of the Divine regardless of whether we are or were aware of its magnificent influence or not. Truly the REAL self is an ongoing love story between the individual and God and the soul keeps sacred its courtship. To properly attend to caring for the REAL self, therefore, is to honor, guard, and heed the authenticity of self inscripted in the deep recesses of the soul. Modern and popular modes of self-help improvement perhaps can only propel to skin-deep satisfaction. Soul-size health calls for a commitment to a journey in faith.

"Gallup polls indicate that only 5 percent of the United States population lack a belief in God. Yet even for believers, faith is a complex palette."[13] Our faith may be in an abstract transcendent

---

[13] Joan Borysenko, *A Woman's Journey to God* (New York: Riverhead Books, 1999), 13.

force or our God may be the Creator of a Divine Plan to which it is our duty to surrender.

No matter what the dictates of our faith may be, real faith is a journey that becomes an evolutionary process.

As we grow and change, tasting the bittersweet realities of life, our faith is likely to change as well. Faith in the God of childhood ripens with the challenges of life. Both victory and defeat temper faith, as do wisdom and love. Along the way it is healthy to undergo periods of question and reevaluation. Have we arrived at our own faith and our own path or simply internalized the beliefs of parents, clergy, spouse or friends? Do our beliefs nourish us and give us the strength and guidance to be better people? Does our faith inspire us to serve life and to make a difference in the world, or is it based on the narcissistic hope that a Santa Claus God will fulfill our wish list if we are good?[14]

The exploration of these adult questions is the true business of how to nurture our REAL self and to release the power in our soul. As with any journey, there are barren spells. Even if we think we are dried up and spiritually dead, Mother God uses these times to draw us closer to Herself, like a loving mother seeking to bring in her children out of some wicked weather. There are no voids for God. Her Presence is everywhere, always. Our faith evolution is illuminated when we can recognize that nurturing the REAL self is one with acknowledging that God is always unconditionally loving and nurturing us, even if it doesn't look or feel that way. Human interpretation is the demon that severs us from true soul messages. Opinion cuts the dialogue of our divinity seeking to heal our humanity. Therefore, true Self/Soul nurturing is a deliberate decision to actively pursue a relationship with the innermost core of our being. Although this sounds hopeless, endless, and random in attempt, it is not.

A major pathway to the treasure chest of the soul is Silence. The act of silence may remind us of some obscure rules found in memories of parochial days. Signs in hallways, then, might have read "Silence in church" or "Be quiet in classroom until you are called upon." In later years, we might have identified silence as something ominous or fearful. Maybe we remember a familiar echo: "Be quiet, kids, your father is sleeping." For some, silence brings forth tension. Our conversation speaks of it. "You are so quiet. What's the matter?"

These examples are not the silence that becomes the vehicle to our soul. Soul silence shuts out distractions so that the Presence of godly awe can speak and be heard loud and clear. Soul silence is the feeling we get when sensing the innate strength of a tree as we simply ponder its splendor. Holy silence is absorbed while sitting in a boat in the middle of a very still lake. Upon an early morning snowfall, the pure white landscape speaks to the soul and its need to

---

[14] Borysenko, *A Woman's Journey to God*, p. 14.

be quiet. And the violet and lavender sunset sends inspiration to its witnesses that lasts deep into the black night.

Our soul is alive and speaking all the time but sometimes worldly priorities isolate us from its rich poetry and muse. Young children embody such holy images and dialogue. Just unobtrusively watch them play or pray! Their purity is as wise as an elder priest or priestess. Yet because of their age, they know not of the wisdom that they "are." Time and development is meant to interpret the young sage so that lessons learned can be applied by conscious choice.

"Spiritual growth is inextricable from psychological growth. And psychological growth is, in part, a gender issue. Men and women are different, our bodies as well as our brains."[15] What remains the same in both is the fact that through the Mother Principle the Presence of the Divine awaits from within to steady the course of maturity and self-nurturing. For men, the journey impels leaving the home, courageously dying to an old self so he can dream his own dreams into a personal reality. For women, the spiritual journey is less a matter of climbing up than of looking in and discovering the Inner Light that has been there all along.[16] Men are meant to bring and build a new world sourced by the message of soul. Women's lives and relationships become the subtle fiber of transformation through their very essence. They teach change by example.

Through the balance of male and female spiritual maturity, the lives of our children and children's children can be dramatically

---

[15] Borysenko, *A Woman's Journey to God*, p. 15.
[16] Borysenko, *A Woman's Journey to God*, p. 71.

healed. With this in mind, whenever we really nurture ourselves, the healing benefits can ripple for generations. No wonder it is such an "awesome" task. Yes, REAL self-nurturing is a blessing for some, yet a curse for others, due to the effort and discipline involved. However, once we commit to the journey, the rewards and spontaneity of a joyful life outweigh all the rest.

There are many ways to adhere to a silent journey within. Some seem ordinary but not less holy. So many times throughout my younger years and adulthood, I have witnessed my mother "in the kitchen." It was her temple place. Often she would sit at the table with a well-worn prayer book quietly reading as she held prayer cards of deceased members of our family. I would come and sit with her and she remained uninterrupted. "What are you doing, Ma?" I would ask. The reply was simple and direct. "Twelve years ago today, Aunt Grace died. I'm going to make pineapple pound cake. It was her favorite. I'm praying for her while I'm doing it." In that holy instant, a shift would occur in my heart. I could hear Aunt Grace's wonderful laugh and see her beautiful face. The fragrant baking ingredients would become incense for my soul. The blessing of that moment would remain with me all day.

Another unproclaimed holy silence would occur when, as a young girl, I would wait for my father to come home from work, and then I'd follow him upstairs. He would ask briefly about my day while emptying the contents of his pockets in a mundane and routine fashion. Invariably, I'd hear the sounds of keys and coins as they found their way to the glass-top dresser. Then slowly he would pause and remove his brown rosary beads from his right-side pants pocket. He would hold them for a second, then kiss them, and then gently place them on the dresser. The beads made no sound. In that single moment, it felt like everything stopped and nothing was important—only to feel the silence and the power of dad's quiet rosary beads. Another moment would pass and dad would smile and instruct, "Let's go eat."

Daily deeds are powerful and can be filled with soul-size feelings, if we can be close enough to God's holiness on a daily basis. Our souls carry God's Love and being close to it lights our steps and relaxes our shoulders. Heavy hearts are hard to carry. By spending daily quiet time, prayerful time through service, reading, cooking, dancing, singing alone or with others, we learn to let God carry us. The art of true self/soul nourishing is epitomized in the expression "Let go and let God." The act of letting go is not to remain passive but only to let go of the burden of fear. We cannot amply achieve this through surface measurements and crisis petitions. Letting go means letting go of the way we think it "ought" to be and to plunge deeper into the silence of our souls where true God awaits in the temple of a quieted heart. To quiet the mind and heart is a call for discipline. I strongly suggest that every day, even before getting out of bed, we begin with moments of quiet breathing and praying. Simple prayers bring splendid grace. "Thank you, God, for this day. Please walk with me; in fact, carry me today so that I might feel You loving me, no matter what." Then again to complete the task-filled day, I suggest moments of quiet again.

"Lord, Mother/Father God, bless me, wash me as I sleep that I might remain clean of heart to follow Your will. Thank you for the blessings today and forgive me if I offended anyone as I forgive whoever may have offended me. Let me and my loved ones sleep, guarded by Your Angels. Thank you. Amen."

As a particular quieting routine takes hold, other types of self-care can enhance the experience of daily life. Once the foundation of inner peace is well connected, ordinary activities can truly replenish the whole person, mind, body, heart, and soul. A lingering bath, a walk in nature, drawing for the fun of it, and writing simple thank-you notes can all revitalize the total being. We can more readily reach peaceful moments since we have not allowed stress to accumulate to exorbitant proportions. Our daily moments of silence have now become spiritual hygiene. We wash away useless worry and frustration, commune with God, and participate in simple pleasures that improve the health of mind and body. We physically feel better, more in the moment, and more lighthearted. We literally don't let the "small stuff" affect us. Every day can then have meaning and value because we do not let ourselves go too far without hearing and feeling the Voice of God.

Unfortunately, this kind of living must be sought after and at first may not even seem normal. Yet at one time, I believe this is how humanity functioned. Perhaps it happened when we were less industrialized and more of an agrarian society. Nonetheless, it is still available if we would seek it.

Sometimes a blessing comes through the mother mold and mother-figure types. We may have been able to learn from these great women in our lives who somehow found a way to shut noisy life out. Maybe we watched someone sit on the porch on a summer night. As we gazed into that person's face, maybe we got lost in the deep pools of her mysterious eyes. Or maybe we watched her painstakingly sew something so that it wouldn't have to be thrown away. Maybe we sat with her as she cuddled a younger child until the child's fever broke.

If you were blessed by witnessing a woman in your life demonstrate unending patience, you were in the company of Blessed Mother God. Her silence may have been painful, but her steadfastness gave new life to any situation.

We need to slow down, be patient with ourselves, others, and with life itself. We need the strong and loving arms of Holy Mother to accomplish this.

If you are ready to slow every part of you down, then I invite you into another healing exercise.

Prayer Room Exercise: In the Quiet, You Are Healed

- Use the same procedure to enter into your Prayer Room as outlined in Chapter One.
- Take several deep breaths and this time really feel each breath go deeper and deeper into your lungs.
- Continue to breathe slowly, witnessing any changes in your body.

- Take your time and observe everything in your Prayer Room.

- If you choose to, add beautiful flowers and a healing fountain; allow for a huge skylight directly overhead.

- Take your time and really sense that you have created a beautiful temple place in your Prayer Room.

- Allow a Radiant Shower of Green Light to enter into your Prayer Room, and let it wash all over you and sense it miraculously even cleansing you inside.

- Focus on the sounds from within your Prayer Room, the shower of Green Light, running water from the healing fountain, and the beating of your own heart.

- Continue to breathe slowly and become as quiet and still as possible.

- Take your time; this experience is not to be rushed.

- Now sense an image of Mother God that you are comfortable with; sense Her dress in magnificent Blue and Yellow Light.

- Sense Her facing you with open arms and pure White Light coming from Her Heart to yours.

- Sense Her inviting you to be held in Her Divine arms.

- If you accept, feel being held in a cradle of Blue and Yellow Light.

- When you are ready, imagine Holy Mother God asking you the following questions.
  - Will you let me love you?
  - Will you let me take away your pain, worry, guilt, shame, and fear?

- Are you ready to walk through your days feeling Me holding your hand?
- Do you believe all is forgiven?
- Do you really want peace in your life?
- If so, then are you ready to spend more time with Me in Holy Silence?

- Take your time and do not judge the experience.
- Allow your SELF to simply remain in the Presence of Mother God, quietly, doing nothing.
- Remaining in silence may be difficult at first, so repeat this exercise frequently until remaining quiet in the Presence of God for 15 to 20 minutes becomes peaceful.
- If various thoughts and emotions surface, don't force anything; simply let them float by without judgment.
- Eventually, the quiet, peaceful time begins to heal and inspire you with great awareness.
- Cherish your quiet times.
- Whenever you are ready, conclude this exercise by saying, "Thank you" and ascending the ten steps of Golden Light back out to outer conscious awareness.

It is advised that you repeat this exercise several times. Your true relationship with God will increase every time. It is also suggested that you write your feelings and/or responses in a journal for further reflection.

Chapter Eight: Ave Maria

Having come this far in the journey of the Mother Principle, it is appropriate to bring forth pertinent reflections regarding our own experiences and inherited impressions about who and what is the true evidence of God as our Mother. Were we raised with the notion of a God as Mother? And if the presence of Mother God was taught to us, did we really understand Her true Power?

Some may project that a Mother God is a greater image of a very loving mother. This is true only in part. If this projection implies passivity and submission, it is totally false. Mother God is the Holy Motivator and Activator of Creation.

Notice again that every culture who uses the Mother God sees Her as proactive. She creates, bears children, and intercepts or protects against evil. Sometimes She has been seen as Kali, the Hindu goddess of retribution and one of Shiva's wives, but She's not usually portrayed to be nearly as ferocious as the male God who seemed to play favorites and was given to every human emotion, such as jealousy, spite, anger, and petulance. Regardless of which way you wish to believe, whether you choose a maternal or paternal God, I think it bears stating here that if God is all-perfect, loving, and omnipotent, how can He or She be filled with petty human emotion? This is not faith. It defies logic.[17]

Mother God and Her expression through the archetype of the Mother Principle is God in action. Mother God is Divine Love in action. Her activities are always unconditional and in holy service to all humanity. True God can do nothing less. Mother God puts into action the eternal love story between God and humanity that includes its trials and victories and whatever it takes to preserve the evolutionary process. Mother God protects and cultivates the Divine promise that we are made in the image and likeness of God and therefore destined to become godlike.

This promise is best demonstrated through the Christian recognition of Mary as Mother of Jesus. Mary (Miriam Bar Joshua) truly understood her divine purpose in carrying out the process of God as she said, "Yes" ("Fiat") to becoming the mother of Jesus. She did so regardless of the circumstances before, during, and after her commitment.

In those days Mary arose and went with haste into the hill country of Judah, and she entered the house of Zechariah and greeted Elizabeth. And when Elizabeth heard the greeting of Mary, the babe leaped in her womb: and Elizabeth was filled with the Holy spirit and she exclaimed with a loud cry, "Blessed are you among women and blessed is the fruit of

---

[17] Brown, *Mother God*, p. 8.

your womb! And why is this granted me, that the mother of my Lord should come to me? For behold when the voice of your greeting came to my ears, the babe in my womb leaped for joy. And blessed is she who believed that there would be a fulfillment of what was spoken to her from the Lord."

And Mary said:

"My soul magnifies the Lord and my spirit rejoices in God my Savior, for he has regarded the low estate of his handmaiden. For behold, henceforth all generations will call me blessed; for he who is mighty has done great things for me, and holy is his name. And his mercy is on those who fear him from generation to generation. He has shown strength with his arm, he has scattered the proud in the imagination of their hearts, he has put down the mighty from their thrones, and exalted those of low degree; he has filled the hungry with good things and the rich he has sent empty away. He has helped his servant Israel, in remembrance of his mercy, as he spoke to our fathers, to Abraham and to his posterity forever."

And Mary remained with her about three months and returned to her home. (Luke 1:39-56)

This highly regarded passage from scripture is known as the prayer called the *Magnificat*. It expresses Mary's vision, purity, faith, and mission within its poetic flow. From the first verse, Mary demonstrates her total union with God as she rejoices, "My soul magnifies the Lord." These simple words are abundantly rich in prophetic metaphors. Firstly, these words illuminate the oneness of God in Mary and her ability to feel His loving presence. Secondly, the verse exemplifies the Mother Principle as the loving nature of God within us who "moves" all events towards Spirit greatness. Throughout Mary's praising prayer, her faith never falters. She says boldly to God, "Yes," I trust You; I love you, Lord; I follow Your will. This act of faith is again exactly how the Mother Principle in us desires to be divinely released the more we listen to it and heed its messages. Mary's response also leaps into an extraordinary vision that transcends time. She acknowledges the presence of the Holy Spirit and appears to be one with its wisdom as she proclaims her place in history as profound and permanent through her words, "All generations shall call me blessed." Again, in similar fashion, this resonates with the significance of the Mother Principle being the change agent within us that can ripple through future generations. What is so powerful about Mary's acceptance of her position in humanity is that it is not arrogant. In fact, she claims it through humility by her words, "He has regarded the low estate of his handmaiden." If we use her verse as metaphor, we can understand true power cannot be found in our human dimension. It is in our spirit nature because God has "called" it to be so. Mary's vision securely states her submission to God's will lifts her into an understanding that as she becomes the mother of Jesus, the birth will change the course of history past, present, and future. From the prophecies of Abraham, God's hand of justice will transform humanity through Jesus because she said "Yes."

Regardless of our faith, or the weakness of it, when we, like Mary, say yes to God, the Christ Consciousness within us is released. This Cosmic Love Consciousness does and will continue to transform humanity back into its divine blueprint with every action of goodness and love. Our universal yes to God recreates our nature into unconditional Mother God love.

The gift of Mary known as Blessed Mother is also shown through another scriptural passage:

At the Marriage Feast of Cana, Mary had an opportunity to keep the love of her Son to herself alone. She had the choice of continuing to be only the Mother of Jesus. But she knew that she must not keep that love for herself alone under the penalty of never enjoying love to the fullest. If she would save Jesus, she must lose Him. So she asked Him to work His first miracle, to begin His public life and to anticipate the hour—and that means His Passion and Death. At that moment, when she asked water to be changed into wine, she died to love of Jesus as her Son and began to mount to that higher love for all whom Jesus would redeem when He died on the Cross. Cana was the death of the mother-son relationship and the beginning of that higher love involved in Mother-humanity, Christ-redeemed relationship. And by giving up her Son for the world, she eventually got Him back---even in the Assumption and the Coronation.[18]

If we allow this scripture reference to speak to our personal lives, the metaphor becomes a megaphone about true love and its selflessness. When we bond with Mother God from within, we soon realize that it cannot be contained. Its holy healing dynamism is meant to be shared. Divine Mother Love gives to all, so that all can be transformed. The Feminine Face of God proclaims wholeness, healing, love, and spiritual power for everyone. She divinely breathes through us for the sake of that power. Holy Mother is power in us, for us, yet never to be used as power over anyone.

As we grow in Mother-humanity bonding, we can realize many petitions and aspirations as truly prayers answered. And just like Mary, we need to learn to pray with our hearts so that our souls can magnify the Lord as well. The more we pray with our hearts, the more God and the law of love make sense. We become eager to live in its precepts. The heart of love is filled with power, action, and miracles. Prayer of the heart is the meeting place for Divine Mother and humanity.

If you are ready to reconnect in your heart and pray with a "magnified" soul, then I invite you to enjoy the following prayer process.

---

[18] Fulton J. Sheen, *The World's First Love* (San Francisco: Ignatius Press, 1952), 163.

Prayer Room Exercise: The Prayer of the Heart

- Use the same procedure to enter into your Prayer Room as outlined in Chapter One.

- Take several deep breaths and allow each breath to become a little slower and a little deeper; allow your entire body to feel completely relaxed.

- Feel a beam of beautiful Blue White Light pouring into your Prayer Room through the skylight directly above you.

- Feel the Blue White Light showering you with waves of endless Peace.

- As the Blue White Light is continuously bathing you, silently in your heart repeat the word "Peace" several times until you can really feel your body, mind, and heart become quiet and calm.

- Now allow an image of Divine Mother that you can accept to be standing directly in front of you.

- Allow Her to open your heart as much as possible. She is directing the Blue White Light to go into your heart now.

- It may feel like the core of your chest is becoming a calm and deep pool of Blue White Light peace.

- Now allow your attention to focus into the Blue White Light pool of peace.

- Keep your attention into the pool of peace and continue to take deep breaths.

- Now Divine Mother will speak to you through the pool of peace.

- Notice Her image now appearing in the pool of peace. Listen to Her speak.

- Divine Mother speaks to you now, by showing you various images in the pool of peace.

- These images reflect experiences in your life when you were called to open your heart more, love more, forgive more, and you may or may not have said "Yes."

- Be silent and watch and listen to Her as She explains the situation for your deeper wisdom and understanding.

- Divine Mother will now give you a choice to love more by showing another image in the pool of peace that reflects a present circumstance in your life.

- Be silent and watch and listen to Her as She explains this opportunity for you to open your heart more.

- Take a few more deep breaths and decide if you desire to finally say "Yes."

- If you choose to say "Yes," watch and listen as Divine Mother shows you through images in the pool of peace the results of you saying "Yes" to letting more love come through you.

- Take your time and remain with Divine Mother as long as you wish to complete the experience.

- Cherish these experiences.

- Whenever you are ready, conclude this exercise by saying "Thank you" and ascend the ten steps of Golden Light back out to outer conscious awareness.

It is advised that you repeat this exercise several times. Your heart will become healed through every prayerful session. It is also suggested that you write your feelings and/or responses in a journal for further reflection.

Chapter Nine: Heaven and Earth Are One

Through the understanding of the Mother Principle, regardless of who our mothers and mother-figure types were, we can begin to reclaim the core of our being. At the center of who we are is the soul, pulsating in Divine Light no matter what. The more that we seek to connect to our core soul, the more we feel God as our Mother. Just as our own biological mothers and mother-figure types began the journey to find inner peace and security, Mother God heals and completes it.

When we approach God as our Mother through prayer and silence, the soul's memory bursts open with all the jewels stored there from Heaven. Reaching the soul releases joy, peace, wisdom, and the desire to celebrate the life we were given. Touching the soul opens Heaven's treasure chest securely placed deep in our hearts. Truly these charisms are always there, yet few seem to simply take the time to go within and let the power of the soul speak to them.

Our daily living no longer makes quiet time, prayer, and soulful reflection a priority, even though if we did we would move through our days with a clearer sense of purpose and direction. We would no longer be burdened by useless fear, worry, and mental confusion. Instead, so many of us watch too much television, become enmeshed in other people's drama, and take our direction from the "latest and greatest" in advertising. It would appear that for many the locus of control and attention is the outer, chaotic world. There is no way for fear to ever be quelled as long as we are stuck in this outer-based reality. It is too mercurial and often rooted in greed and force. These can never be the attributes of our true and loving God.

Security and safety are the innermost expressions of our soul. Our relationship with Divine Mother cultivates these qualities. When our hearts are calm and we know our truth, we are no longer obsessed with fleeting measures of peace and illusions of love. Whenever we feel frightened or insecure for any reason, we become defensive. Psychologically, this is a normal reaction. Yet when this posturing becomes more repetitious and eventually fixed, we lose our ability to be happy and open. We begin to mistrust others, ourselves, and life itself. This habitual response to daily living separates our senses from feeling the power and promises in our soul. The more we feel disconnected, the more our day-to-day living can feel like hell.

Many people live in their own private hell. Loneliness, poverty, grief, and resentment fracture the natural lifeline of peace that the soul and Mother God have to offer. Separated persons create splintered families and communities. Disproportionate fear and anger can escalate into nation against nation. In fact, if we look at the world, it would seem to be so.

Conversely and positively stated, the effort for world peace is somehow still etched upon the heart and soul of humanity. Mother God will never abandon us. She will never take away Her power and promises to keep us safe, secure, and evolving. We, however, need to go to Her. Her magnitude doesn't have to be created; it needs to be released from within us.

As certain as our breathing, so too is God. Mother/Father God is everywhere, totally and completely! My own heart swells as I recall the words of Thomas Merton, whose prayer and poetry state such praise.

> There is no leaf that is not in Your care. There is no cry that was not heard by You before it was uttered. There is no water in the shales that was not hidden there by Your wisdom. There is no concealed spring that was not concealed by You. There is no glen for a love house that was not planned by You for a love house. There is no man for that acre of woods that was not made by You for that acre of woods. But there is a greater comfort in the substance of silence than in the answer to a question. Eternity is in the present. Eternity is in the palm of the hand. Eternity is a seed of fire whose sudden roots break barriers that keep my heart from being an abyss.[19]

Our fears create the abyss that keeps us falling into confusion and despair. We were never designed to be abandoned. It is a complete and divine impossibility. Instead we are constantly

---

[19] Thomas Merton, *Dialogues With Silence* (New York: Harper Collins, 2001), 89.

cradled. Holy Mother's arms are always around us and we can feel
Her care only as we remain connected from within.

> You formed my inmost being.
>
> You knitted me together in my mother's womb,
>
> You know me through and through
>
> My being was no mystery to you
>
> When I was formed in secret
>
> Woven in the depths of the earth. (Psalm 139)

As we allow this passage to soak in, the realization of divine truth
can arise. God is with us, in us, like an ever-present, loving Mother. We
are eternally safe. Heaven is within us! Only the frightened mind is the
trickster whose devilish ways want us to believe differently. Again
Thomas Merton's words bring forth power and truth.

> Minds which are separated pretend to blend in one another's
> language. The marriage of souls in concepts is mostly an
> illusion. Thoughts which travel outward bring back reports
> from You from outward things, but a dialogue with You,
> uttered through the world, always ends by being a dialogue
> with my own reflection in the stream of time. With You
> there is no dialogue, unless You choose a mountain, circle it
> with clouds, and print Your words in fire upon the mind of
> Moses. What was delivered to Moses on tablets of stone, as

the fruit of lightning and thunder, is now more thoroughly born in our souls as quietly as the breath of our own being.[20]

In the quiet of our hearts, we can remember and reclaim Heaven. And through our union with Divine Mother, we can move Heaven into earth. Once we experience the inner safety coming from Divine Mother, we can change our motivations for daily living. Ordinary tasks, challenges, and crises do not have to scatter our peace. Staying inwardly connected sustains peace and wisdom. Our perceptions shift. We are no longer engaged in inner or outer battles. Heaven is always close. We feel it. We hear it and we follow its directions. The union of Holy Mother of the heart is just as much of a heavenly experience as when we were safe and secure in our mother's womb. Our prayers with silence feed us like an umbilical cord to God. This is how God intended it to be.

The more we focus on Heaven in the heart, God's abundant love can readily be felt. We want to be happy, sing, and share it with others. Kathleen Norris says it best in her book, *Amazing Grace*:

Let us sing alleluia here on earth, while we still live in anxiety, so that we may sing it one day in heaven in full security. We shall have no enemies in heaven, we shall never lose a friend. God's praises are sung both there and here, but here they are sung in anxiety, there in security; here they are sung by those destined to die, there, by those

---

[20] Merton, *Dialogues With Silence*, p. 93.

destined to live forever; here they are sung in hope, there in hope's fulfillment; here they are sung by wayfarers, there, by those living in their own country. So then, let us sing now, not in order to enjoy a life of leisure, but in order to lighten our labors. You shall sing as wayfarers do. Sing, but continue your journey. Sing then, but keep going.[21]

As we steady our paths by calming our hearts, we can take action with our lives. From the simplest deeds to the most challenging decisions, our center can no longer be shattered. Our inner calm is our rudder, and Mother God continues to steer it. Our reality alters. We feel our true self. Opinions have faded, negativities and falsehoods have been washed away. Every day now carries newness and vitality. Through union with Holy Mother, we are re-born yet mystically we remain Her children forever. She encourages us to sing and dance, play and pray with our lives. Regardless of our cultural diversity, our Divine Mother loves all Her children, male and female alike. Her heartbeat pulsates Divine Love in us and through us. It is Her Presence that makes us gather together for the sake of miracles. When we embrace the power and significance of who is in our souls, Heaven is expressed in our exhales.

Individually and as families and communities, we need to accept the Heaven of the heart and bless every tiny deed with its grace. "Hear, O Israel, the Lord our God, the Lord is one; you shall love the Lord your God with all your heart, with all your soul, and with all your

---

[21] Kathleen Norris, *Amazing Grace* (New York: Riverhead Books, 1998), 368.

mind and with all your strength. The second is this; you shall love your neighbor as yourself. There is no other commandment greater than these" (Mark 12:28-34). When we commit to love God, we commit to acting differently. It is in the assistance necessary to act differently that Mother God offers us Her greatest gift. We can change earth into Heaven. And we do not have to do it alone. Our Holy Mother is always ready to hold us, heal and direct us, if we would but ask Her to do so! It is not only possible, it is promised to be so.

As we conclude our journey here, I invite you to "ask" your Holy Mother to make your life truly heavenly, safe, and secure.

Prayer Room Exercise: Ask Your Holy Mother

- Use the same procedure to enter into your Prayer Room as outlined in Chapter One.
- Take several deep breaths and allow each breath to become a little slower and a little deeper.
- Take your time; let each breath bring you deeper and deeper into the core of your being.
- Sense an image of Mother God that you can accept.
- Sense Her as dressed in royal and heavenly garments.
- Sense Her as the Mother of the Universe, Womb of Creation, the High Priestess of Humanity, the Healer of the Heart.
- Ask Her to lift you into another dimension so you can feel like you are with Her in the Garden of Paradise.

- Take a few more deep breaths and allow Her to take care of you as She carries you into the Garden of Paradise.

- Relax as you sense yourself with Divine Mother in the Garden of Paradise.

- Use all your senses and feel the beauty, the balance and safety of earth as it was intended to be.

- Ask Her any questions that you would like.

- Be grateful and reverent. This is a blessed experience.

- Now allow Her to take you to a special place in the Garden.

- She has a gift for you. Holy Mother will now take a gift that was hidden in a beautiful tree and hand it over to you.

- Trust your first impressions. You may ask Her anything about the gift to enhance your understanding and acceptance.

- She will now press the gift into your heart so you will always have it.

- Now relax and take a few more breaths.

- When you are ready, and if you choose to, ask Holy Mother this question: "What can I do in my life that would help to make Heaven come to earth?"

- Relax, take your time, and trust your first impressions. Accept your experience.

- Now feel Holy Mother place one hand on your head and one on your heart. Feel a deep sense of peace and love flow through your entire being.

- Relax and enjoy Her loving you.

- Take another deep breath and sense Her, in the silence of your heart, speak to you: "You can make a difference, if you choose to let me help you."

- If you desire to, you may respond, "Yes, Holy Mother, I ask Your help, Your refuge, and Your love."

- Trust now it is done. You are bonded to Her care forever. You are safe.

- Bless and cherish these experiences.

- Whenever you are ready, conclude this exercise by saying "Thank you" and ascend the ten steps of Golden Light back out to outer conscious awareness.

It is advised that you repeat this exercise as you desire. With each experience, you will feel more loved. It is also suggested that you write your feelings and/or responses in a journal for further reflection.

In Your Blessed and Loving arms, we are safe. Heal us, Mother God. Keep us in Your Heart as we shall keep You in ours. Thank you. Amen, Amen, and Amen.

Bibliography

Baynes, H. G. *Mythology of the Soul*. London: Methuen, 1949.

Borysenko, Joan. *A Women's Journey to God*.
New York: Riverhead Books, 1999.

Bradshaw, John. *Creating Love*. New York: Bantam Books, 1992.

Brown, Sylvia. *Mother God*. Carlsbad, CA: Hay House, Inc., 2004.

Estes, Clarissa P. *Women Who Run With the Wolves*.
New York: Ballantine Books, 1992.

Forward, Susan. *Men Who Hate Women and the Women Who Love Them*.
New York: Bantam Books, 1987.

Johnson, Elizabeth. *Dangerous Memories*. New York: Continuum, 2006.

Lanzetta, Beverly. *Radical Wisdom*. Minneapolis: Fortress Press, 2005.

Maloney, George. *Mary: The Womb of God*.
Denville, NJ: Dimension Books, Inc., 1976.

Merton, Thomas. *Dialogues With Silence*. New York: Harper Collins, 2001.

Neumann, E. *The Great Mother: An Analysis of the Archetype*.
London: Routledge & Kegan Paul, 1955.

Norris, Kathleen. *Amazing Grace*. New York: Riverhead Books, 1998.

Sexton, P. C. *The Feminized Male*. New York: Random House, 1969.

Sheen, Fulton J. *The World's First Love*. San Francisco: Ignatius Press, 1952.

Sprinkle, Patricia H. *Women Who Do Too Much*.
Grand Rapids, MI: Zondervan Publishing House, 1992.

Stevens, Anthony. *Archetypes*. London: Routledge & Kegan, Ltd., 1982.

Teresa, Mother. *In the Heart of the World*.
New York: Barnes & Noble Books, 1997.

Walsch, Neale Donald. *Conversations With God, Book I*.
New York: G. P. Putnam's Sons, 1995.

To my Mother, Julia K. Grancagnolo
January 14, 1920 – April 15, 2005

Oh mother, mother of mine
How I long for your touch,
But you are gone.
How I long for your touch
And the lingering of your scent.
Yet you remain vanished.
Despite the decades of days and days,
All linked together in endless
Memories of all you taught me
All you gave me and all you took.
Yet you remain gone, just gone.
A single second separated us.
One blunt moment halted
All the past of who we were.
Days and decades of loving,
Longing for loving, all halted now.
Death has created our days
Endless again; I remain longing
For your touch, to feel your hand
In mine telling secret stories,
In the silence of our clasp.
I longed for your touch then and now;
Yet you are gone, and days and decades
Must pass until the silent hands
Can finally be and forever be
Rejoicing in the celebration of our loving.
Then our hands will be clapping
And applauding, free and safe, sharing
All stories, more stories, even making new stories.
Yet for now, I long for your touch,
That sleek, tiny hand that told me so much.

By: Ginger